The Kicking Game

The Kicking Game

**Ben Agajanian
and
Paul T. Owens**

**Foreword by Tom Landry
Head Coach of the Dallas Cowboys**

Celestial Arts
Millbrae, California

Celestial Arts
231 Adrian Road
Millbrae, California 94030

First Printing, August 1980

Cover design: Jim Kelly

Made in the United States of America

Library of Congress Cataloging in Publication Data

Agajanian, Ben, 1919-
    The kicking game.

    1. Kicking (Football)   I. Owens, Paul, 1942-
joint author.   II. Title.
GV951.7.A32   796.332'27   80-66071
ISBN 0-89087-267-8 (pbk.)

1 2 3 4 5 6 7 8   86 85 84 83 82 81 80

Foreword

With the importance of kicking in football, it is only natural for a team to have a player who does nothing but kick. The game is becoming so sophisticated and specialized that soon there could be a player for each type of kick. Greater specialization adds the dimensions of more excitement and better individual performance to the game.

As the value of the kicking game increases it becomes almost imperative for a team to have a kicking coach. Realizing the need for such a coach and teacher, the Dallas Cowboys hired Ben Agajanian 15 years ago to only work with kickers.

Ben had the right credentials. He was the NFL's first kicking specialist when he played for the Philadelphia Eagles and Pittsburgh Steelers in 1945. In his twenty-year career he kicked for many teams and was one of the best long-distance kickers in the game, establishing numerous team, stadium and league records. As a kicking coach, he is unsurpassed. Most people can tell you that you missed the kick because you hooked it to the left. Ben can tell you why you hooked it and what you can do to correct it.

The subtle things he has done to improve our kickers has helped us in many team efforts. He takes kicking quite seriously and is most effective at adapting his knowledge to influencing any kicker and any kicking style. I would call him the top authority in the field of kicking.

This book is a must for every kicker and for kicking coaches. Even head coaches. I urge anyone who wants a comprehensive guide to the fundamentals and techniques of kicking to read this book.

Tom Landry
Dallas Cowboys

Dedication

This book is dedicated to all kickers and potential kickers. I deeply hope that it will help them in developing and improving their own art of kicking.

I want to thank God for giving me the physical and mental talents to teach myself how to kick.

Ben Agajanian

Contents

Foreword *by Tom Landry* 5

Introduction *by Ben Agajanian* 9

History 11

The Mental Game and the Coach 17

The Kicking Game Today 25

General Instructions 32

The Punt 33

Kick-Off, Soccer-Style 47

Kick-Off, Straightaway 53

Field Goals, Soccer-Style 59

Field Goals, Straightaway 65

The Center and Holder 71

Conditioning for Kickers 81

Records 89

Ben Agajanian

Introduction

Kicking a football is an art, and I want you to enjoy it. If you learn the proper techniques, you will kick better and want to kick more.

This book is designed to help you learn and to improve the kicking game at all levels of competition. My intention is to teach you in a simple and basic way. This is a *how to* book. All that has to be added is your *discipline, concentration,* and *dedication.*

To be disciplined you must follow instructions and be coachable. You have to be ready to react in game situations as you have been taught in practice. If you are disciplined, you will.

Total concentration, mentally and physically, on what you have to do will make your kicking a natural part of your athletic skills. By dedication I mean devoting much of your time to practicing kicking and keeping yourself in top physical shape. In order to be a successful kicker you must sacrifice activities that would hinder you from performing to your potential ability.

You do not need luck. You can be as good as you want to be.

Ben Agajanian

George Blanda wins another one: Overtime against the Washington Redskins, score tied, seven seconds remaining, fourth down on the 16-yard line—the Oakland Raiders win, 26-23, on the Blanda field goal.

History

The kicking game has been affected by major changes throughout the history of football. The most influential have been:

1. The emphasis placed on running and passing.
2. The shape and size of the ball.
3. The position of the goalposts on the field and the distance between each post.
4. The point value of the scoring kick.
5. The reliance on the kicking specialist.
6. The attitude of coaches towards kicking.

Organized American football began in colleges in the 1860s as a modified version of soccer and English rugby. Players could only advance the ball and score by kicking. Games were played with an over-sized, egg-shaped ball.

The rules of the Intercollegiate Football Association in 1876 allowed for running with the ball but emphasized kicking. A touchdown merely gave a team the right to try for a kicked goal. A successfully kicked goal after a touchdown counted six points. A missed kick after a touchdown was worth four points. A field goal counted five points.

Some college leagues in this era of sports counted three touchdowns equal to one field goal. A team that scored three field goals could have six touchdowns scored against it and still win the game. Other leagues played with a touchdown

and a field goal worth the same. By 1897, college rules con-
formed:

Touchdown	6 points
Field Goal	5 points
Extra Point	1 point
Safety	2 points

In 1909, with the expanded use of the forward pass, the
field goal dropped in value to three points.

Each play from scrimmage began with the center snap-
ping the ball back with his feet to other players. The center
was in the middle of all players, and as Walter Camp, the fa-
ther of American football describes, "By pressing suddenly
downward and backwards with his toes, he could drag or
snap the ball to the man behind him."

The dropkick was very popular while the design of the
ball was wide without the pointed ends of today's football.
The longest dropkick on record was 65 yards. George Gipp,
the famous Notre Dame player drop-kicked a ball 62 yards in
1916. The kick for extra point was once tried from five yards
out and directly in line to the goal-line point where the touchdown was scored, or the scoring team could "kick-out"—
punt the ball to a place where the angle was more feasible for
a successful extra point attempt.

Jim Thorpe, one of the best all-around football players
both in college and the pros, kicked at an average of 60 yards
per punt and was often successful on 40- and 50- yard field
goal tries. His coach, the legendary Glen (Pop) Warner
described the average player of the early 1900s as knowing
"what to do with his toe."

Although the great running back and kicker, Ernie
Nevers, set a field goal record in 1926 of five in one game—a
record that held for forty years—kicking was on its way to
losing scoring priority with coaches.

Teams were too involved with developing and perfecting
their running and passing offenses to devote much time to re-

Jim Thorpe

fining the kicking element. The most respected coaches of that time, Knute Rockne, Pop Warner, and Howard Jones were strictly offensive-minded. Rockne brought the forward pass into prominence. He did not use kicking as an offensive weapon, but merely as a defense—a means of sending the ball out of danger when forced to give up possession.

Pop Warner championed the first down. He felt that the team with the most first downs should be given credit on the scoreboard. While he was inventing the hidden ball play, the running guard, and the unbalanced line, the kick was relegated to further unimportance. Howard Jones built a sound offense, a system based on possession of the ball. He used the quick kick as a surprise offensive tactic. The quick kick was considered easier to perfect and more deceptive than the attempting of a punt.

Coaches who followed these legends were all out for the touchdown. Kicking was considered a last resort, a derogatory action. The irony, of course, is that after teams had fought unsuccessfully to score the touchdown they had to rely on kicking to make the difference between winning and losing.

The size of the ball changed drastically in 1934. It became more streamlined, favoring the passing and running games. This meant the virtual end of drop-kicking. Players had less control of a dropped ball because of its narrow shape and sharp points.

The goal posts have been narrowed, and widened, put on the goal line and end of the end zone—all in the name of increasing or decreasing the value of the field goal and extra point.

In 1932, the National Football League's championship game was played indoors in Chicago because of blizzard conditions. The arena had enough room only for an 80-yard field. The goal posts were moved from the end line to the goal line. The following year it became a league rule. In 1934, Jack Manders of the Chicago Bears set a single season record of ten field goals. From 1933 to 1937 he converted on seventy-two consecutive extra point attempts. In 1974, the NFL followed the high schools and colleges and moved their goal posts to the end line.

The distance between each post of the goal posts was originally 24 feet in college. It was changed to 18'6" in 1931 and 23'4" in 1959. The year after the increase in 1959, there were 103 more successful field goal attempts in college ball.

Unlimited substitution and an increase of the number of players on a team's roster has allowed the game to have kicking specialists. Free substitution meant that a player could come into the game just to kick. He did not have to play any other position. With the larger team roster, coaches could have one, two, possibly three or four players as kicking specialists. There could be a kicker for each type of kick.

The first coach to take advantage of utilizing the kicker to maximum was Paul Brown of the Cleveland Browns. In the late '40s and throughout the 1950s he appreciated the potential of the field goal and his kicker, Lou Groza, led the NFL in field goals for five seasons. The important point to consider here is that the Browns used the field goal as a strong offensive weapon. It was not relegated to last chance maneuver for the Browns. Part of the team's working strategy was to work the ball down the middle of the field for the attempted field goal.

Groza, however, doubled on the team as a tackle. Other great players who were part-time kickers just as football was nearing the kicking specialist era were Paul Hornung, Gino Cappelletti, and George Blanda.

Placekicking entered a new phase with the introduction of the soccer stylist. The first American college soccer-style kicker was Pete Gogolak, of Cornell. In his first year in the pro ranks, with the Buffalo Bills in 1964, Gogolak kicked 45 out of 46 extra points and made 19 of 28 field goal attempts. With his success, coaches from other teams sought soccer-style kickers. To get them they had to go out of the country, and by the 1970s teams had players from Norway, England, Austria, Germany, Armenia, and Hungary.

The advantages of soccer-style kicking are that the kicker gets more of his foot to hit the ball than does the straightaway kicker. This allows him to have more control of his kicks. It also makes it possible for him to put more power into the ball—more of his body force can meet the ball through soccer-style kicking than kicking the straightaway method. Along with the power and control, the soccer-style kicker can get more distance on his kicks than the straightaway kickers. But, there is no disadvantage to straightaway kicking. For extra points and short field goals it is a perfect method. Straightaway kickers can get a higher trajectory in the first five or ten yards of their kicks than soccer-stylists.

The top five lifetime leaders in scoring in the National Football League have had extensive kicking careers. And all of them have gotten their kicking points through the straightaway method. The longest field goal is by a straightaway kicker, Tom Dempsey, 63 yards.

Whatever the method, whoever the coach, the kicking game has often been the most important element in football.

The Mental Game and the Coach

The mental attitude is one of the most important aspects of kicking. You cannot kick well unless you have confidence. A coach can help make or break a kicker's confidence. The coach must be on your side if you are going to be successful.

If the coach comes up to you after you have missed a kick and says, "That's OK, you'll get it next time," or "Try it this way next time, and you'll make it," he is building your confidence, by encouraging you. A coach who does not like his kicker's progress should either encourage him to do better or get rid of him. If a kicker does not feel he is respected and has the confidence from his coach, he has no incentive to improve. And, more importantly, he will not want to do well.

Kickers do not need negative criticism, just positive encouragement. Coaching is building of confidence. The best attitude for coaches to have is, "While he's kicking, he's my favorite kicker." The kicker must feel that he is an important and integral part of the team—all the time. If a kicker does not kick as well in games as he does in practice, he can be helped by having workouts with heavy rush drills. This will train the kicker to react under pressure much as he will during a game.

You can reduce your kicking nervousness and tension during a game by warming up on the sidelines. Kick a ball into a practice net, or have the center and holder practice in front of you, and follow through without kicking the ball. If

17

you go a long time without kicking during a game, warm up anyway. Stay ready.

When you are called into the game, concentrate on lining up and getting ready to kick. Do not start telling other players what they are supposed to do. Emotional slapping on everyone's behind is not necessary either. And, remember, the holder is responsible for lining up the ball, not you. *Concentrate.*

The players on the other team may try to distract you by talking to you or yelling to other players. Learn not to listen. Once I had a string of extra points completed which was one shy of a record. The other team knew it and yelled to me, "Aggie, we're not even going to rush. We're going to watch you set the record."

I started thinking about what they said. I wondered what they were going to do, and I forgot about my kicking. They were telling the truth, though. When the center snapped the ball and the holder placed it down, none of them rushed. I was so preoccupied with what I thought they might do that I looked at them when I kicked the ball, and it went way off to the side. No record, and all because the other team was more important than my kicking.

A consistent and effective form is also very important. You want to kick the ball with a natural stride. You cannot go slow one time and rush the ball on the next kick. If you do, you will lose a sense of consistency.

The only time you should change your approach for a field goal is when attempting kicks which are exceptionally far for you. To get extra distance in your kick, put more quickness into your kicking leg. Do not think about kicking the ball harder to get it further, or taking an extra step. Think quickness! Bring your leg and body through the ball quicker. Quickness, a smooth rhythm, and a fast follow-through are your major strengths as a kicker.

Do not hold back when you kick-off. Be aggressive but stay in control. I have told kickers who were too cautious— fearful that the ball would go in a line drive, be hooked or not go far enough—to imagine that the ball was someone or something they did not like. It always worked—they met the ball more powerfully.

As for what kicking form your coach should have you use, I give you the conversation I had with a kicker who came to me at a pro training camp:

"How do you want me to kick, coach? Your way or mine?"

"I don't care. You kick the way you want."

"But somebody said I won't make the team unless I kick like you."

"You'll be our kicker if you kick better than anybody else who's trying out."

I like to cultivate a kicker's style, not change it. I can give him advice, watch him in practice and, if he does not use my suggestions but does well in the game, that's fine. But if his way is not going well for him, I will have to work on getting him to change. His basic form, however, I will not change, especially on the college and pro levels.

Although it is difficult not to take a coach's suggestions personally, remember he is just trying to help you. A coach who knows about kicking and why you have been missing is only talking about the truth, not about you personally, as evidenced by this conversation I had with a rookie pro kicker.

"How did I do, coach?"

"Lousy. You didn't kick too well."

"You don't like me, coach."

"That's not true. I like you. It's your kicking I don't like."

After I explained why he had not kicked well, I asked him, "Did you like your kicking?"

"No."

"Well, then we agree."

But be easy on yourself. Some of the kickers who did well in college but never made it in the pro ranks are still kicking. No matter if you are kicking for a team in front of millions who are watching on television or you are doing it on a field all by yourself, kicking is controlled more in your mind than off the top or side of your foot.

Compensation

I do not like for kickers to compensate, that is, try to make up for something they cannot do naturally or over play to a certain set of circumstances.

Kickers who tie the tip of their shoe to their ankle with a string in order to lock their ankle are a good example of compensation. They are compensating for the fact that they cannot or will not lock their ankle naturally when they are kicking. When they do this, they are causing their plant foot to come closer to the ball. In order for them to be effective with their string locked ankle, they will have to have the ball tilted towards them. When the ball is tilted back, it is more difficult to hit it in the right spot for good distance and height. What usually happens to kickers who kick this way is that they will either kick the ball too close to the bottom or top of the ball. The result will be the ball will spin more, not go further.

A kicker can compensate when he has sliced the ball. He will overreact to the kick on the next attempt by hooking it in the other direction. And, if he hooks one, he will slice the next one as a way of overcompensating and making sure he will not do the same thing again. The best way not to compensate in such a situation is to forget about the missed kick and concentrate on doing it the right way next time.

Weather is a natural excuse for compensating. Some kickers will take an exaggerated step and hook the ball to compensate for windy conditions, when all that has to be done is for the holder to counter the wind by leaning the ball into the wind, or positioning his hold so the kick will head into the wind. The wind will not carry the ball out of line if the head of the ball is leaned into the wind by the holder. The kicker does not have to create any compensating approaches.

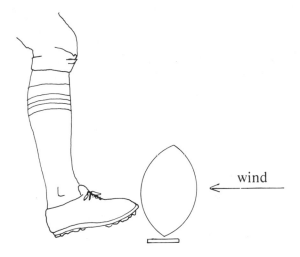

wind

Atmospheric Conditions

In most areas of the United States, in the beginning of the football season, the air is light. This means the ball will travel further on punts, kick-offs and field goal attempts than it will during mid-season when the weather is cold. In the colder weather the ball will not hang in the air as long.

When kicks are affected by the cold, kickers usually make the erroneous assumption that their leg is getting tired, that it is "dead." Kickers blame their lack of distance on not being able to hit the ball hard enough, when the weather is the reason for their shorter kicks.

In enclosed stadiums the kicker is at a slight disadvantage because the air is thicker than in an open stadium, but he can benefit from the lack of wind and the warmer air.

There is no way to make up for the loss of distance you get kicking in cold climates. Just be more patient with yourself on those days, and remember, that sticking your foot in front of a heater on the sidelines or wearing electric socks to compete against the wind and cold may make you feel better, but will not help you kick the ball further.

Excuses

Over the years I have heard almost every type of excuse made by kickers when they have missed. What I have always been fascinated by is how the blame is never theirs. Kickers are not responsible for the missed field goal, but for some reason they are not afraid to take the credit when they make one.

The List of Kicker's Excuses
1. Bad center.
2. Bad hold.
3. The weather was too cold.
4. My feet weren't warm enough.
5. The ball was too muddy.
6. The ball was too soft.
7. The ball was too new.
8. The goal posts looked too narrow.
9. The goal posts looked crooked.
10. I didn't look at the ball 'cause a girl was walking behind the goal posts.
11. I wasn't ready.
12. The holder didn't tell the center when to snap the ball.
13. My leg (toe, back) hurt.
14. My head hurt because the helmet was on too tight.
15. I was too nervous.
16. The players didn't want me to kick; they wanted to try for touchdown.
17. I had to go to the bathroom.
18. My socks were too dirty.
19. The laces on the ball weren't facing the front.
20. My shoe laces weren't tied.
21. The center took too much time and broke my concentration.
22. It was a strange field; I've never played on a field like that before; you can't get the ball to go anywhere you want it to.

23. I got a bug in my eye.
24. My left hand got in my way.
25. The wind didn't move the ball well.
26. My shoes were too tight.
27. The coach didn't give me enough time to warm up.
28. The holder's knees got in the way.
29. The ball was upside down.
30. The grass was too high (we were on Astro Turf).

There is no best reason. There does not have to be. No matter how true any of these are, they do not count on the score board. Even if they are true—a few are—the best way to forget about it is to take the bad feelings for having missed the kick and turning those feelings into excitement for the next opportunity.

Ishmael Ordonez, University of Arkansas

The Kicking Game Today

The importance of the kicking game in football today can't be overemphasized. Taken totally—kick-offs, punts, place-kicking—it is the equal of the offensive or defensive contributions. It is not surprising, then, to find a team using its most talented and dedicated athletes on kicking teams. It should be impressed upon the members of these "special teams" that it is their responsibility to establish effective field position. In order to do this, each member of the kicking team must be well-trained, disciplined, and understanding of what is expected of him, and able to execute his duties effectively.

Kick-off

The ability to kick the football into the end zone on the kick-off is a wonderful attribute. However, there are other qualities most coaches feel are essential. For instance, if the kicker is consistently able to kick the ball inside the ten-yard line with a hang time of more than four seconds, his team has an excellent chance of stopping the ball carrier inside the twenty yard line. Additionally, by making the receiving team return the ball, the defending team has an opportunity to create a fumble.

The kicking team must always anticipate a return. If the ball is not returned, the ball is *free;* that is, whoever covers the ball takes possession at that point.

25

The kicker leads the team downfield; any member of the team who is ahead of the kicker at the instant the ball is kicked will be penalized for being offsides. The kick-off spot—40 yard line for high school and college, 35-yard line for pros—requires a maximum effort and a five-yard penalty only makes it that much more difficult to place the ball near the goal line. The kick-off is from the 40-yard line in high school and college, and from the 35-yard line in the pros.

The kicker, in addition to the obvious task, is responsible for making sure all eleven men are on the field and prepared to go before signaling the referee. He also may be required to place the ball to a particular receiver, or away from a returner, or to an area of the field which will cut down on the return possibilities.

Standard responsibilities:

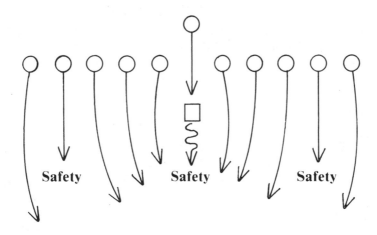

In order to confuse the receiving team's blocking, defenders may reverse their order on the downfield routes:

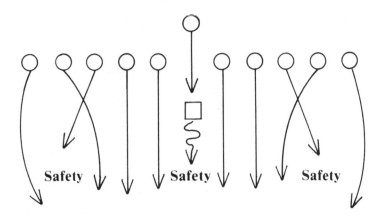

The Onside Kick

A short kick which travels the required ten yards, is a free ball and belongs to the team that attains possession of it. Intentionally kicking the ball short in an attempt to cover it before the receiving team is called an *onside* kick. If the ball is recovered by the kicking team, it cannot be advanced.

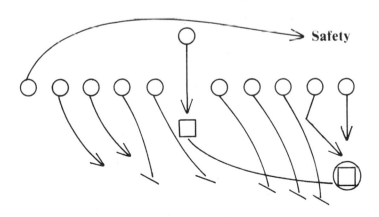

There are several techniques of kicking which, when well-executed, will give the kicking team an additional advantage.

The Spin Kick: This is achieved by kicking the ball with the instep so it slices or hooks, drastically. The maximum spin of the ball causes it to travel back toward the kicking team after having traveled approximately twelve yards.

The Tip-Off: The ball is kicked a few inches below the top so that it will bounce and turn over, making it difficult for the receiving team to recover. It is usually kicked to one side or the other, but can also be used straightaway when the receiving team is not expecting an onside kick.

The Over-the-Line: The ball is kicked softly in a high arc to clear the first line of players on the receiving team—not too high or someone may be able to run under it, not too long or the kicking team will not be able to cover it quickly. If the receiving linemen are reluctant to run back to block, looking for the 12–15 yard kick, the kicking team has the possibility of running through them and recovering the ball.

The Straight-Out: When the receiving team is anticipating an onside kick, to one side or the other, it is often more effective to kick the ball to midfield. The kicker approaches the ball slowly, kicking away from the front line men, following the ball quickly, and after it has gone 10 yards, recovering the ball himself.

The Squib: Used to prevent or eliminate a possible long return before the end of each half. The ball is placed flat, on its side, on the tee or on the ground. A strong kick directly into the side of the ball will cause unpredictable bouncing and an extremely difficult to field and return ball.

*Note:*If the ball does not go ten yards, players on the kicking team should fall on it immediately. If they do not, the receiving team will recover and the ball will belong to them at that spot. When the kicking team recovers the ball before it goes ten yards, they have the opportunity to try another kick-off, after a five-yard penalty.

Punt

Surrendering the ball to the opposing team is not a good idea, but when fourth down comes up, it's comforting to have a consistently effective punter. As in kicking off, distance is important, but not the most important unless the hangtime is also good. The optimum among the top kickers is a little over five seconds. Anything less than 4.0 seconds can be tragic.

Another element to consider is the speed with which a kicker can get the ball away. The receiving teams, even on a planned return, will have men aggressively trying to get to the punter and block the kick. Generally, the time taken to punt should be no more than slightly over two seconds—two and a half seconds is *too slow*.

Standard responsibilities:

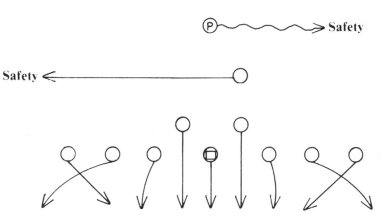

The movement of players downfield is delayed until the punt is away; individual blocking assignments would, of course, depend on the defensive alignment and game situation.

Another punt formation commonly used:

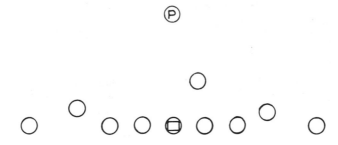

This formation is particularly effective when attempting a fake punt; it allows four possible receivers to get free quickly.

Field Goal/Point-After-Touchdown

These kicks have a special importance because they are offensive weapons that directly affect the score. The execution must be quick and perfect since the ball is being kicked only seven to eight yards behind the line of scrimmage. The time it takes the kicker to get the ball away from the time the ball is snapped should be less than one and a half seconds.

Standard formation:

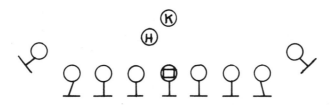

Blocking responsibilities are foremost on a field goal and downfield coverage takes place—on long field goals—after linemen hear the thump of the kick. Notice that blocking is tight and to the inside; the idea is to make a defender run all the way outside to get to the kicker, while keeping defenders in the center from penetrating close enough to intrude into the ball's trajectory.

General Instructions

We are wording the instructions for the right-footed kicker. Left-footed kickers should use the same directions, just change the words *right* to *left,* and *left* to *right.*

When directions say for your foot to be so many inches in front, behind or alongside the ball, you count from the top of your shoe. For instance, your plant foot should land six to eight inches ahead of the ball, means that the first six to eight inches of your shoe will land in front of where the ball is placed.

Adjustments on your steps should be made depending on the length and size of your legs. Obviously, a tall kicker will take longer steps than the shorter kicker. When we say your feet should be 4–6 inches apart, or your foot should be to the left and 8–10 inches behind the ball, etc., all the distances vary according to the size of the kicker and the length of his leg.

The Punt

Introduction

A *punt* is a kick from scrimmage which surrenders the ball to the other team. It is usually attempted on a fourth down but can be tried on any of the four downs. Punts are made when teams do not want to take the risk of trying to make a first down running or passing, when they have exceptionally poor field position, and when they do not want to risk losing the ball on a fumble or intercepted pass.

The punt is an important defensive weapon and can be a very offensive one. If one team can outkick an opponent on the average of ten or twelve yards a punt, it will have a distinct advantage. The team with the poorer punting performance gives its opponent better field position.

Ray Guy, Oakland Raiders

Instructions

1. Stand twelve (high school) or fifteen yards (college and pros) behind the center. While you await the snap of the ball from the center lean over slightly, have your arms outstretched, palms open and your fingers pointed upward at your chest level, giving the center a target, just like the catcher gives the pitcher a target in baseball. Keep your eyes on the ball and follow it all the way into your hands.

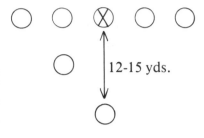

12-15 yds.

2. Your right foot should be slightly ahead of your left. Your weight is evenly distributed on the balls of both feet, with slightly more weight on the right than on the left. Four to six inches separate each foot.

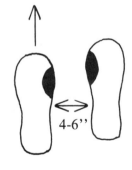

4-6"

3. With one continuous motion catch the ball in the center of your body at approximately waist level, bring it into your waist, step off with the left foot. Align over your right leg; hold the ball in that alignment throughout your approach to the ball. When you catch the ball, turn it so that the lace is on the right side and the valve is facing up.

4. Stride forward with the right foot, the ball is chest high and directly over the kicking foot.

5. Stride forward with the left foot and push the ball out ahead of you. Drop the ball so your kicking foot meets it approximately two feet above the ground or at the level of your knees.

6. As you drop the ball, drive your kicking foot up through it.

Explanation

1. High school punters stand twelve yards back because this distance is adequate for protection. Also, it is often difficult for a high school center to snap the ball fifteen yards accurately. College and pros stand back fifteen yards because the rush is faster than in high schools.

2. Your weight is leaning forward when you begin your approach so you will get more distance and height into your kicks. If your body is straight up or leaning backwards when you kick, you will have a tendency to kick the ball in a line drive.

3. The lace and valve sections are the dead part of the ball. (The lace is made of string, leather, or rubber. The valve, which is used for inflating purposes, has a hard rubber bladder beneath it.) Kicking the ball in either of these places will lessen your kicking force, take away from your kicking control, and keep you from kicking a perfect spiral.

4. To control your kick, your kicking foot and the ball must be aimed in the same direction. The front end of the ball, the end pointed away from you, must be directed downward and turned in. When your toe meets the ball, it is also pointed down. You are trying to get most of your foot on the football. The best way is for the curvature of your foot to fit the shape of the ball. To get a spiral on the ball you must point the nose of the ball down and in. If the nose is pointed up, the ball will go straight up.

Take a ruler and measure two feet off the ground, or place your hand on your knee and step back, letting your hand stay suspended where the knee was. On that line, real or imaginary, is where you want to kick the ball.

Timing is of utmost importance. If your kicking leg is slow on the upswing, you will have to drop the ball from a higher level so you meet the ball at the right place. A kicker with a quick leg can drop the ball lower than a kicker who is slower in his kicking time. If you drop the ball lower than knee level, you will kick it on a line drive. If you hold the ball too long and kick it from a high place, it will go straight up.

Hold the ball higher to get more height, but not as far out as your arm's length. To get more distance into your kick, hold the ball further out and a little lower than you usually do. If you drop the ball lower, you will get less hang time, but it will go further.

There are two basic ways of holding the ball before you kick. One is with both hands, the other with one. With both hands, your left hand is around the front of the ball, your right hand is around the back. The left hand is for support, the right hand is for directing the ball. You can also hold your right hand underneath the ball, although I wouldn't recommend it. It is a matter of personal choice. The ball is always held at arm's length.

The second way is for your right hand to do all the holding just before you kick. This method is recommended for kickers who have a wide grip. Kickers who use this approach feel they get more momentum and have more balance when their other arm is free to swing as they step into the ball.

Do not stand still while you turn the ball to where the lace is on the side and the valve is up. Do the turning while you are making your steps to kicking the ball. In this way, you will not lose time in getting the kick away.

If you keep the ball aligned in the center of your body, your tendency will be to turn to the right on your first step and on your kicking step you will cross your kicking leg sharply to the left, causing the ball to hook to the left and taking at least ten yards off your distance. If you hold the ball to the extreme right, beyond your leg, you will slice it off the side of your foot.

Your footing can be with a two- or three-step approach. The two-step approach is right foot, left foot, and kick. The three-step approach is left foot, right foot, left foot and kick. This approach is recommended for younger kickers, as it will give more control of the kick.

Hang Time

A long hang time allows for good team coverage on the punt return. The object with all punters is to eliminate the possibility of a punt return. Or, if there is one, that it be short. You increase hang time by holding the ball closer to your body.

A line drive with a hang time of four seconds or less will not allow your team members to cover adequately. Such a situation can net the other team a substantial return, even six points. You want to get enough hang time to allow players to get down the field to where the returner is waiting.

Suggested excellent hang times:

4.5–4.6—high school and college kickers

4.8–5.0—professional kickers

A good punt must be high as well as long. Good timing will add distance. Good timing and a small amount of power in your swinging leg will do more for you than poor timing and a great deal of power and force into your kick. Just like with golfers, good timing and control is more important than power in driving a ball.

Timing of the Kick

The coach should time how long it takes the kicker to get his kick away after the snap of the ball. In general, punting times for high schools and colleges are:

Up to 2.2 seconds—very good

2.3–2.4 seconds—good

2.5 seconds—too slow

For the pros:

Up to 2.1 seconds—very good

2.2 seconds—good

2.3–2.4 seconds—too slow

If there is a heavy rush, the time will be one-or two-tenths faster because you will be rushing the kick.

Bad Snaps
and Other Unfortunate Situations

To recover a bad snap, get your body in front of the ball. If the ball is rolled or bounced back to you, cross your left knee in front of your right leg to block it and pick it up. Do it as if you were a shortstop picking up a fast ground ball. Do not spread your legs. If you do, the ball may go straight through. If the ball is snapped to either side of you, try recovering it with your body in front of it. Do not stick out your right or left hand to catch the ball. You will have a better chance of catching the ball with your body in front of it.

If the ball goes over your head, do not jump up to get it. It is too easy to bat the ball around, fumble, or come down with it to find yourself surrounded by the opposing team. Back up quickly and reach for it. If you see that it is going too high to catch it this way, turn around and run after it. Do not back up to retrieve a long overhead snap; the ball may still get over your head, or you may not be able to gain control of it before a member of the opposition tackles you. Practice bad snaps to improve your reaction time to the unwanted situations.

Do not kick the ball if it is clear that the ball will be blocked. Run away from the players who are too close, and if you are able to get clear, kick the ball, if not, run. It is better to have control of the ball and be tackled with it, than to allow the momentum of the defense to deflect it and recover for their own advancement.

Do not waste your concentration by looking for players coming to block the ball. Do not think about them. Concentrate on kicking the ball. If they should be there before they're expected, you will know it. After you kick, they are always going to be there.

Out-of-Bounds and Direct Spot Kicks

To kick the ball out-of-bounds or to a specific place or player, turn your body to where you want the ball to go. Do not step straight ahead and then hook your leg across your body on the last step trying to place the ball there.

A punt which goes out-of-bounds across the sidelines will be placed in-bounds at the point, where it crossed the line and the receiving team will take possession at that point. If a punt goes into the other team's end zone and is downed there, or goes out-of-bounds through the end zone, it is a touchback. This means that the receiving team will take possession of the ball on its twenty-yard line. If a player on the receiving team touches it, and the kicking team recovers it, the ball belongs to the kicking team at the spot of recovery.

The Wind

To punt into the wind, hold the ball lower than you usually do. Hang onto it longer and drive the ball into the wind. This will make for a line drive up with a good spiral. The natural aerodynamics of the ball will cause it to carry higher and hang up longer than usual.

To punt with the wind behind you, hold the ball higher than you usually do. You want the kick to have maximum altitude and let the wind carry it. Dropping it from a lower position will lessen the wind's effect on the ball.

Training Methods

The "rocker step" kick can be useful for training. It was a standard kick in football in the 1920s and 1930s—a step and a half kick that was a good method for the quick kick. It allowed the kicker to be closer to the line of scrimmage, nine yards back or less, thereby letting him get the ball off sooner than punters of today. When you begin this kick, both feet are together, or the left leg is slightly forward. As you receive the ball, step back with the left foot in a rocking motion, then step forward with the left foot and kick with the right.

If you have a tendency to step to the right on your first step, practice by punting from between two pieces of tape. The pieces should be six feet long and three feet apart. This will help train you to start and finish your kick on a straight line.

Remember: Excellent form makes for consistency. Consistency makes for an excellent kicker.

Things to Think About

A punter, like any other kicker, must be concerned with kicking with his body, not just his leg. You will have an excellent punt if your body is forward, bent over slightly, your shoulders are straight and tilt back slightly as you kick and your leg comes up high in your follow-through.

To guarantee you will kick correctly, you must concentrate on kicking with your entire body, not just your leg:

1. Keep your eye on ther ball and head down.

2. Your shoulders are square and aligned with the goal post.

3. Your feet are four to six inches apart, right foot in front of the left when you await the ball.

4. When you step to kick, the ball is aligned with your right leg.

5. Your knee and ankle are locked and kicking toe is pointed down.

6. Your kicking leg is straight and comes up high after you kick the ball in the follow-through.

7. Your left leg (the plant leg) will come off the ground naturally in the follow-through.

The punt is part of one motion.

Quick Kick

A punt done when the receiving team does not expect it is called a "quick kick." It is used to get the ball further down the field, beyond the safety who is playing up close to stop the running or passing play. The object is to put the receiving team in a poorer field position that would be achieved if the kicking team used its regular punt formation, and the receiving team had its usual punt coverage.

The kick is made from a close formation, where the kicker is five or six yards behind the line of scrimmage. It is done by the kicker taking the snap from center, stepping back with his left foot, keeping most of his weight on his right foot, striding forward with his left foot, and kicking with his right.

Some kickers are able to take a very short step with their right foot, just before stepping forward with their left, and kicking through with their right foot.

Kick-Off, Soccer-Style

Introduction

A soccer-style kicker approaches the ball from a right angle position and kicks it with the instep of his foot between the toe and ankle. The method is popular because of the control the kicker has of the ball and the height and distance he can achieve with it. Soccer-style kickers also get slower spin on their kicks, allowing the ball to travel farther. Kickers who use this method are also able to get much body strength into their kicks, resulting in more distance.

There is no one perfect way to kick the ball in the soccer-style method. Only basic fundamentals about this kicking form can be learned. A kicker's style is developed by the natural way of swinging the leg and entire body through the ball. Just because you like a particular college or pro team, and their kicker is your favorite player, does not mean that you should kick like he does. You may both be soccer-stylists, but your forms can be entirely different.

Coaches at the junior levels, from grade school through high school competition, can modify a kicker's form and style. Once a kicker gets to college and the pros and has been relatively successful, his basic style should not be changed. Some minor alterations or modifications as to positioning, posture, etc., can be suggested for improvement, but avoid changes that require the kicker to develop different movements during execution.

Instructions

1. Back up ten yards behind the ball in a straight line and move five steps over to the left at a 90° angle. Put your left foot in front of your right, four inches apart. The upper part of your body is leaning over so that your weight is balanced slightly forward. Your eyes are looking at the ball.

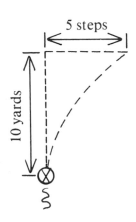

2. Start your approach slowly with your right foot, and take small steps for the first five yards. When you begin the second five yards, pick up your momentum, increase your speed.

Rafael Septien,
Dallas Cowboys

3. Keeping your eyes on the ball, plant your left foot approximately six to eight inches to the side of the ball (off a two-inch tee), two to four inches behind the ball, and hit the ball with your right foot just below the center of the ball. Make sure the ankle of your kicking foot is locked and your toes are extended forward as you kick the ball between your toe and instep. Swing your hip through the ball on the follow-through with your leg, causing your left leg and body to lift off the ground.

Efren Herrera, Seattle Seahawks

3. Run the first five yards slowly and evenly to get your rhythm and body momentum under control. In the second five yards run at the ball with more speed to make it go high and long. You want to *attack* the ball in order to kick it with power.

4. If your plant foot is closer than six to eight inches to the ball, you will have a tendency to hook it. If your plant foot is farther than six to eight inches away, you will have a tendency to slice it. Your body's follow-through will cause the ball to go further and higher.

Remember: Quickness makes power. Kicking with your leg and following through with your body makes for greater height and distance.

Off a one-inch tee the left foot is planted six to eight inches beside the ball and two to four inches in front. Off a two-inch tee your left foot should be six to eight inches beside the ball and two to four inches behind the ball. Off a three-inch tee your left foot should be six to eight inches beside the ball and six to eight inches behind the ball.

The hang time for soccer-style kickers on a kick-off at all levels of competition is judged as follows:

4.2 seconds—excellent
4.0 seconds—very good
3.8 seconds—good

Explanation

1. Start your approach from ten yards behind the ball to give you enough distance to build up to ultimate momentum by the time you reach the ball. Ten yards back will allow you to hit the ball with quickness in your body and leg. You move five steps over to the left to give you the angle you need to get your hip and body into the kick at maximum speed.

2. Your weight is balanced slightly forward so you will kick the ball with your body over it. This will ensure greater distance and height than if you kicked with your body straight or leaning backwards.

Kick-Off, Straightaway

Introduction

This traditional method of kicking off developed from the concept that the toe was the best way to meet the ball with your foot, to kick straight and lift it up. Shoes used for straightaway kicking were the usual round-tipped toes. During World War II, however, the square-tipped shoe came into use. It was an advantage over the regular football shoe in that the square tip allowed more of the shoe to meet more of the ball. This gave the kicker more control of his kicks, and enabled him to have more power in his kicks.

Instructions

1. Stand ten yards directly behind the ball and align yourself with it and the middle of the downfield area.

2. Place your right foot approximately four inches in front of your left, lean slightly forward with a little more weight on your right foot than your left, and put your eyes on the ball.

3. For the first five yards of your approach to the ball your steps are slow and even. On the second five yards you will pick up momentum to kick the ball with the force of your entire body. Plant the left foot four to six inches to the left of the ball and 12 to 18 inches behind it. Drive through the ball with your entire body.

Explanation

1. Line up directly behind the ball to get the straightest and shortest distance to the end zone. Usually you will want the ball to go into the end zone. If you want to kick the ball to a specific spot other than the end zone, aim for that spot—and run in a straight line towards it when you approach the ball. Do not run up to the ball and try to hook or slice it in the direction you want it to go. Aim in straight, start in that direction and kick it straight. Do not kick it out-of-bounds. By keeping the ball from going out-of-bounds you keep your team from being penalized five yards and having to kick over again.

Line up ten yards behind the ball to fully utilize the quickness and strength in your approach. Ten yards gives you enough distance to get the full force of your body into the ball.

2. Your body is leaning over in order for you to continue in that position when you kick the ball and follow through. Your body over the ball when you kick will ensure greater distance and height than if you kicked the ball with your body in an upright position or leaning backwards.

3. You are kicking with your entire body, not just your leg. The first five yards are run slowly and evenly to get rhythm and body momentum together. In the second five yards your speed is increased so that by the time you plant your left foot by the ball you are ready to attack it. *Attack it!* Get mad if you have to, but kick the ball with power. If your rhythm and

Ray Guy, Oakland Raiders

timing are right, you can control your attack of the ball, making it go high and long. *Hint:* If your right foot lands at the five-yard mark behind the ball on your approach, you should be in step.

Your left foot should be four to six inches to the left of the ball, and the following distance behind the ball when you kick.

Off a one-inch tee—12 inches
Off a two-inch tee—14 inches
Off a three-inch tee—18 inches

These distances vary, however, according to the size of the kicker and the length of his leg.

Kick-off hang time at all levels of competition—high school, college and professional:

4.2 seconds—excellent
4.0 seconds—very good
3.8 seconds—good

Kick-off points are:

High school—the 40-yard line
College—the 40-yard line
Pros—the 35-yard line

The Tee

The Kick-Off Tee
This is an aid to hold the ball upright, at the desired angle. There are one-, two-, and three-inch tees. Most of them are made of rubber or plastic.

Before the three-inch tee in pro football, kickers used a one-inch tee and wrapped two inches of sponge beneath them to raise them higher. One- and two-inch tees are used in high school and college games. The professional kickers use the one-, two-, and three-inch tees.

There are some general pointers to note about the tee.

• The higher the tee, the more height you can get out of your kick (if you kick correctly).

- If you kick the tee and the ball together, you will lose many yards on your potential distance.
- Kickers coming into pro football should not hesitate to use the three-inch tee, even though they have had success with the lower tees in high school and college.
- The ball should be placed as straight as possible on the tee. Do not slant or lean the ball drastically on the tee. This will cause the ball to spin more, but not go as far.

Ishmael Ordonez, University of Arkansas

Field Goals, Soccer-Style

Instructions

Soccer-style kicking for the extra point and the field goal is basically the same.

1. For both types of kicks the ball is placed in the middle of the field or anywhere between the marks, depending on the spot marked at the end of the preceding play. From any placement, align yourself with the middle of the goal posts, the tee, and the center. Take three natural steps from where the holder will put the ball down. Then move over two steps to the left, in a straight line, forming a 90° right angle.

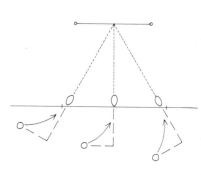

2. Keep your head down and eyes on the spot or tee where the ball is to be placed. Put your left foot in front of your right—four inches apart—with the upper part of your body leaning over so your weight is balanced slightly forward. Don't lock your knees.

3. Start your approach with your right foot and move toward the ball as soon as the holder catches it from the center. The first step is short.

4. The next step, the left foot, is in regular stride towards the ball, building up body momentum. Assuming you are using a two-inch tee, plant your left leg six to eight inches alongside the ball, your toes even with the tee.

5. Follow through with your kicking leg coming through the ball with the force of your entire body.

Explanation

1. The right angle you form is important for your approach. It gives you enough space, within the time allotted, to kick the ball accurately and bring your leg through the ball in the proper arc and swing. If you move one step over instead of two, you will hook the ball when you kick it. If you move three steps over, you will slice it. Optimum body power for the kick can best be realized from this distance and angle.

2. Your weight is leaning forward when you begin your approach to the ball so you will have body balance and get a quick start. Your body is leaning over so you will get more distance and height into your kicks. If your body is straight or leaning backwards when you kick, you will have a tendency to turn your shoulders and hook the ball or kick a line drive. If you are leaning back *too* far, the ball you kick will not go over the line of scrimmage, and you will have a greater chance of slipping.

3. Your first step is short to begin your rhythm. Plant your left foot six to eight inches away from the ball. If you plant it closer, you will have a tendency to hook your kick. If you plant your left foot further away from the ball, you will have a tendency to slice it.

   Using a one-inch tee, your left foot is six to eight inches from the ball and two to four inches in front of it.

   Using the ground, your left foot is six to eight inches from the ball and six to eight inches in front of the ball.

Note: To accomplish the longer kick all you have to do is get more quickness into your leg through the ball. You *do not* approach the ball faster—just keep the same rhythm in your approach and bring your kicking leg faster through the football for that extra power needed to get the ball further. Soccer-style kickers should not approach the extra point attempt too quickly. If they do, they will have a tendency to hook the ball.

Timing:

The time to get the ball kicked is calculated from the time the ball is snapped to when it is kicked. Practice has shown that there is a difference in the speed with which the kick is made during a game.

In a game the center will snap the ball back faster. The holder will set the ball up quicker and the kicker will move to the ball faster than in a practice kick.

For high school and college teams the times are:

In practice—1.4 to 1.5 seconds

In games—1.3 to 1.4 seconds

For pro teams the times are one-tenth of a second faster.

Do not expect the same time in practice drills as you do in game situations unless your practices are done with a heavy rush.

Remember:

- If your left foot is too close to the ball, it will hook to the left.
- If your left foot is too far away from the ball, it will slice to the right.
- If your left foot is too far in front of the ball, your right foot will come in too low and the ball will go too high and you will lose power.
- If your left foot is too far back, the ball will be kicked too low.

The Holder's Tee

This is a tee used for extra points and field goals. It is beneficial for both the holder and kicker. It gives the holder a spot to place the ball. It gives the kicker a spot to concentrate on. It gives him higher elevation and distance when he kicks the ball. It is not permissible in pro ball.

Field Goals, Straightaway

Instructions

1. Take three natural steps back from the two-inch tee, align yourself with the goal post and the tee. Your right foot is approximately four inches in front of your left; your body is slightly forward with a little more weight on your right foot than your left.

2. As soon as the holder catches the ball, begin your approach taking a short step with your right foot, a larger step with your left.

3. Plant the left foot four to six inches to the left and eight to ten inches behind the ball. Kick the ball with your right foot.

4. With your ankle locked firmly in a walking position, your right leg bent at the knee, kick the ball an inch below the center with your toe—the surface of the shoe tip—and follow through by locking your knee and swinging your leg straight up above your waist.

Explanation

1. Taking three steps back allows you to develop momentum but is close enough to allow you to beat the defensive rush. Starting from that point you will have better timing and accuracy than if you began closer or further back from the ball.

2. Your right foot is in front of your left and your body is bent over to help you get a quick and balanced start.

3. Your first step is small to keep your balance and to facilitate a smooth movement into your kicking stride.

4. If you lock your ankle, you will have control and power in your kick. Kicking with your ankle not firmly locked is like hitting a nail with a loose-headed hammer—you will not make strong contact.

Do not lock your ankle with your toes up. If you do, your heel will hit the turf and you will kick the ball higher than just below the center of it. Do not lock your ankle with your toe pointed down or the toe will hit the turf, and you will have a poorly directed kick.

Follow through with your body, and ankle still locked, and you will get more height and distance on both field goal and kick-off attempts. If you do not follow through with your leg above waist level, the ball will have a tendency to fade to the right or left depending on the wind and weight of the ball. A ball kicked with a strong follow-through will travel more accurately and to a further distance.

Straightaway kickers do not have to worry about slicing the ball if they kick it squarely. If you approach the ball too quickly on extra points, you will kick it lower and it will have a higher trajectory. If you approach it too slowly, you will kick it in the middle and the ball will have a lower trajectory, but, hopefully, it will be high and straight enough to get over the crossbar.

Try to get your toes to meet the ball an inch below the center of it. The ball will spin slower than if you kicked it from a lower spot. If kicked lower, the ball will spin faster but will not go as far or with as much accuracy.

If you are kicking from a two-inch tee, kick the ball a couple of inches farther back than where you would kick it from the ground. Kicking from the ground you want to be six to eight inches away from the ball when you bring your foot up, with a two-inch tee eight to ten inches.

Remember: Lock your ankle parallel to the ground, not raising or lowering your foot. Do not dip your toe forward or your foot will hit the turf. Do not lift your toe up in the air or your heel will hit the turf.

George Blanda, Oakland Raiders

The Center and Holder

The Center

The player who centers the football for placekicking, and punting, is not necessarily the same player who gives the snap to the quarterback on plays from scrimmage. Not only are the requirements substantially different, but the regular center may have hands and arms taped, as do other interior linemen, that hinder a smooth delivery of the ball to the holder, or punter.

The Holder

Any player who has quick hands and has the time to practice with the center and kicker could be the holder. Time in practice is important. A first-string quarterback in college or pro football would not be the best candidate for holder—he does not have enough time to develop a perfect routine with the other two in the kicking game.

It is not good for the kicker to have one holder in practice and a different one in the game. He will not have the confidence he needs in the man who is holding the ball. Also, the center and holder need to practice alone, as well as with the kicker.

Instructions

1. The center assumes a lineman's stance with the ball directly in front of him at arm's length. Shoulders are square to the line of scrimmage, head is down to look at the holder or punter.

2. The ball is grasped with the right hand, the fingers across the laces. The left hand is placed on the upper left side of the ball for guidance. The longer the snap, the more the ball is pointed toward the ground.

When centering the ball to the holder or punter, the ball should rotate so that it is received with the laces facing up. This is accomplished by experimenting with the speed and the spin of the ball.

The ball can be held in a flat position for the snap to a holder. For punts, approximately twice the distance, the ball is held at a slight angle in order to get a quicker snap at the wrists. (The smaller your hands, the closer to the tip you will hold the ball.) *Note:* There is some variation as to the amount of movement a center can give the ball prior to the snap; know the rules for your level/area before practicing extensively.

3. The holder kneels seven yards back from the center in high school and college games. It is advisable in the pro ranks for the holder to be seven yards-two feet, or eight yards back, because the linemen are taller than in high school and college. The high school or college kicker has a higher trajectory because he kicks from a tee; the NFL does not allow an elevating tee.

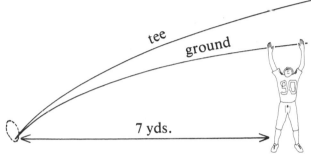

4. One of the easiest and most adaptable ways to align yourself as a holder is to have your right knee touching the ground and your left up. When awaiting the ball, your hands should be held out above the tee. If you extend your hands further out, you will have a tendency to misplace the ball. If you are not allowed to use a tee, as is the rule in pro ball, your left hand is placed on the ground where you will place the ball, and your right hand is held up as the target for the center.

5. When the ball is snapped, catch it with both hands.

6. Find the lace and begin turning the ball until the laces are aimed towards the center. The lace section of the football is the dead part and will reduce your potential distance and height if the ball is kicked there.

7. Start turning the ball as soon as you get it. You do not have to wait until you have placed the ball on the tee or the ground. It is not imperative for extra points attempts that the laces be facing the center, but it is desirable. The kicker can make the ball go up and over from that short distance without the laces in front. Sometimes the holder does not have time to turn the laces for an extra point because it tends to be kicked quicker than a field goal.

8. The hand you hold the ball down with (one finger only) is not the hand which does the turning. If you are comfortable holding the ball with your right hand, then do your turning with the left. If you want to hold the ball with your left hand, then do your turning with the right. *Do not panic.* If you catch the ball for a field goal attempt and know you cannot get the laces completely around to the front, just try to make sure they are not facing the kicker. Part of the way is better than none.

Stand the ball up straight. Do not tilt it in either direction—to the right or left—and do not lean the ball back towards the kicker or forwards towards the center. The theory of leaning the ball to enable the kicker to get more height and distance is a myth. All a lower-angled ball ever does is to spin more than a ball kicked from the straight up position. The only thing fast spinning ever does is take away some of the potential distance of every kick. The only exception is when there is a tremendous wind coming across the field, or kicking into a headwind.

Grading

Symbols for Describing Each Kick

Symbol	Description
↑	Good
⇑	No good
↖	No good, to the left
↗	No good, to the right
↓	No good, short
↑	Good, but wobbly
⇑	No good, and wobbly
D	Dud
Tr	Turf
H	High—long arrow
L	Low
LD	Line drive
S	Short
Hk	Hook
Sl	Slice
↖	Good, but to the left
↗	Good, but to the right
↓	Under the goal post, or short

Grading the Center and Holder

Each member of the kicking trio—the center, the holder and the kicker—are of equal importance in determining the outcome of every kick.

Good pro kickers have lost their kicking edge when separated from a good holder and center. Kickers grow accustomed to a holder and a center and lose some of their own confidence when new people are brought into the kicking unit.

The center and holder should practice their roles in the kicking game as much as the kicker does. Some of that practicing can be done without the kicker. A grading system will help centers and holders feel their importance in the kicking team, give them an incentive for improvement and show the coach who is the best player for each position. I have devised a grading system for centers and holders, as well as for kickers.

Extra Points and Field Goals

Excellent   The ball comes back to the hands of the holder with the laces facing forward and in a spiral.

Good   The ball comes to the hands but the laces are not towards the front.

Fair   The ball is catchable but is too high, too low or too wide to the left or right. It is also wobbly.

Poor   The ball hits the turf before it gets to the holder. It is uncatchable in time for the ball to be placed for the kick.

Punts

Excellent   The ball comes back to the punter's hands quickly with a spiral.

Good   The ball comes back to the punter's hands slightly low, high or to either side of the punter. The ball is wobbly.

Fair   The punter must move slightly to catch the ball.

Poor   The ball rolls on the ground or goes over the punter's head.

Holder

Excellent   The holder puts the ball exactly on the spot on the ground or on the tee with the laces facing front. The ball is straight up and down, and the kicker has sufficient time to kick it.

Good   When the holder puts the ball exactly on the spot or on the tee, but the laces are not facing forward.

Fair   When the holder is slow putting the ball exactly on the spot or on the tee, and the head of the ball is leaning, not straight up.

Poor   When the holder fumbles the ball.

Note: If it is a poor snap, chances are it will be a poor hold. If you have the greatest kicker in the country, he cannot possibly be the greatest if he is working with a poor or fair center and holder.

Coaches often blame kickers for having missed a kick when it was the holder's or center's fault. The complaint is, "You kicked it too slow." The answer for this is, kickers kick it too slow because holders and centers work too slow. If the center and holder do not get the credit for making the kick a success, they should not get the blame for an unsuccessful attempt.

Grades can be totaled each week, or more often on a chart such as the following:

Field Goals and Extra Points

	KICK 1	KICK 2	KICK 3	KICK 4	KICK 5
center's name	E	G	F	G	P
holder's name	E	F	F	G	E
time of kick	1.3	1.4	1.4	1.5	1.3

Remember: Kicking in practice will be slower than in the game.

A coach will want to time a kicking unit to keep it within a specific timing and consistency. The clock helps make the center, holder, and kicker get closer to and stay consistent with a smooth and natural rhythm.

The clock is also used to practice for kicking protection.

Ray Guy, Oakland Raiders

Conditioning for Kickers

Fallacy: Lifting weights to develop muscles will make you kick further.
Truth: You will have stronger legs, but you will not have helped your kicking. In order to strengthen your kicking leg—kick, kick, and kick.

Off-Season Conditioning

During the *off-season* keep yourself involved in a functional strengthening program to develop your arms, shoulders, and legs. This includes a weight-lifting program and isometric exercises. The emphasis, however, should be on:
1. Stretching
2. Kicking
3. Running
It is best that youngsters between the ages of seven and fourteen do little or no weight training.

To help keep your legs in shape, play tennis, racquetball, handball, or other games involving extensive running.

Kicking During Off-Season

Kickers should work out an average of four days a week. Because of the punishing effect kick-offs have on the leg, only twenty a day should be attempted. Punters should kick forty to fifty times during each workout. Field-goal kickers, twenty-five to thirty times for each workout, with at least ten of those counting as extra point attempts from the ten-yard line. If you have two-a-day practices, these numbers apply for each workout. These suggestions are, of course, relative to your age and the condition of your kicking leg.

Weights During the Season

During the season kickers should do no strenuous weight exercises. Just a light program for maintaining muscle tone. Pre-high school kickers should do no weight training during the season or off-season.

Running During the Season

Youngsters should warm up for kicking by running. After they kick, they should run more, a minimum of a half-mile before practice and after. High school kickers should run at least a mile before and after their kicking. The running or jogging will keep from over developing any group of muscles used for kicking. It will offset any muscle strain put on the kicking leg. Running also keeps kickers from pulling muscles. Slow running, that is. No sprints, please.

College and professional kickers should warm up by running a mile before each of their workouts. A mile, at least, is good for the cooling out period after the workout.

Kicking During the Season

Young kickers should kick twenty-five times a day, or until they lose the fun of it. Their friends, parents or coaches should mark off their distances, clock their hang times and grade their field goals, punts, and kick-offs. The high school kicker should do no more than thirty kicks a day during each practice. Towards the end of the week the number should taper off to a half-dozen, two days before the game, and none on the day before the game.

For the college and pros, the kicking practice is relative to what kind of kick as well as the time during the week. A field-goal kicker should do twenty-five per practice, twelve kicks two days before the game and none on the day before the game. The kicker who is practicing kickoffs should do a maximum of ten a day, tapering off to six kicks two days before the game, and none the day before the game. The punter can kick twenty to twenty-five times per practice, twelve kicks per practice two days before the game, and none on the day before the game.

To help the kicker's condition for the game, the coach should not schedule kicking drills the day or two before the game. Heavy rush practices for the kicker can be scheduled any day but the last two before the game. A sore leg will mean an even sorer leg and sorrier score.

On the list of *Definitely Not's,* the following are included for during the season:

- No handball, racquetball, tennis or other heavy stop-and-start competitive games.
- No body-building.

Stretching During the Season

Young kickers do not have to be concerned with exacting stretches and isometric exercises. Push-ups, sit-ups, and the stretching of the feet and leg muscles are the only exercises necessary.

High school, college, and pro kickers should be involved with basic isometric manipulations and the stretching of the hamstring and groin muscles in particular. Upper body stretching is important, but not as imperative as stretching in the area of the legs.

You want to have flexibility throughout the season, but you do not want to get your muscles fatigued.

In order to develop and maintain top kicking ability, it is necessary to develop a daily routine of exercises that stretch and flex the leg muscles. Just as conditioning and weight training must be determined individually to achieve maximum effect, flexibility is a matter of age, size, and physical condition.

The exercises that follow are representative of the many that can be done for not only conditioning purposes, but for warm-up prior to kicking practice and prior to games. Remember when attempting these exercises, or any exercises, that you will not be able to reach the optimum point on the first attempt. Give yourself ample time to attain a greater degree of flexibility—depending on your body type, you may not be able to ever reach the same degree of flexibility as others. This seemingly limited ability, can be overcome by developing strength and quickness. Accept your body's limitations; attempt to extend them gradually—and continue to work to extend them.

1. A basic exercise is one many of us do every morning as we get out of bed: Stand relaxed with legs spread shoulder width. Starting at the toes, begin to extend the body toward the sky.

Raise the body on the ball of the foot, then the ankle, the calves, the knees, the thighs—as you begin to stretch the torso, slowly raise the fingers, hands, arms, above the head. At full extension, the entire body is reaching, balanced on both feet, for the sky, equal effort from both arms.

Bring the arms down and relax. After several slow renditions, do several crossbody extensions—standing with your weight on the left leg, reach for the sky with the right hand, reverse the procedure several times.

A variation of this exercise can be used to strengthen the foot and ankle: When in a fully extended position, move up and down on the feet. Do not bounce; move slowly down with the heels touching the ground, then back up on the balls of the feet. This can also be done with the crossbody extension.

2. Lying flat on the back, arms loose at the sides, bring one knee at a time to the chest. Wrap your arms about the knee and hug it tightly. Return the leg to the ground and repeat with the other leg. This exercise may be done from a standing position also.

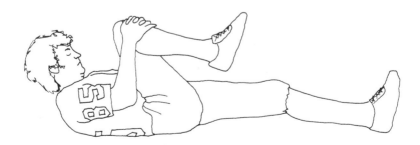

3. Sit with the right leg extended in front of you, the left leg bent at the knee, the foot alongside the left buttock. Reach toward the foot with both hands; grasping the leg at, or near, the ankle pull the body gently down toward the foot. Do several repetitions with both legs.

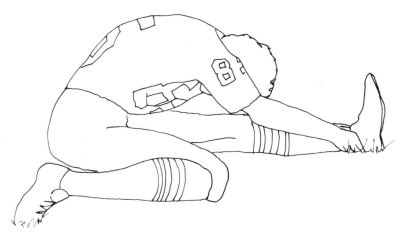

4. Sit with both legs extended in front, spread at a 45° angle. Slowly bend the knees, bringing the feet in toward each other. Grasp each ankle and pull the feet together at the crotch. Release and repeat.

5. Stand with feet spread at shoulder width, hands stretching up. Bend at the waist until you can lean into the ground, forming a pyramid with your body. Slowly and with short steps, begin to walk toward your hands, keeping legs straight and arms and back forming a line. Move back and forth several times—don't force it.

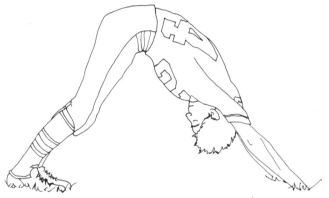

6. Stand with feet spread very wide, arms at sides. Turn the torso to face the right, also point the toes toward the right. Bend the right knee, keeping the left straight, and place the hands on, or near, the ground. Return to a standing position, facing the front, and repeat to other side.

7. Stand with feet spread wide, use arms for balance. Slowly squat. Maintain balance until reaching a sitting position—knees bent at a 90° angle—then bounce gently several times. Return to a standing position, relax, and repeat.

8. Touching the toes. There are many versions that can be valuable. The following is the best for kickers, in my opinion.

Cross the right foot over the left, bringing them as close together as possible. With hands overhead, thumbs interlocked, bend at the waist and reach for your toes. Reverse and repeat.

The kicker must develop other exercises for conditioning the rest of the body, but a combination of several of the above or similar exercises is necessary for developing and maintaining maximum kicking ability.

It is important, particularly at the high school and college levels, to participate fully in the team conditioning program. It's easier to stay in top condition when you are part of a group, but it also improves morale and spirit, making the kicker an accepted, integral member of the team.

Records

PATs (Point-After-Touchdowns)
COLLEGE
Most
Game: **13** by Terry Leiweke
Houston, 1968

Season: **60** by Efren Herrera (in 64 attempts)
UCLA, 1973

60 by Rich Sanger (in 64 attempts)
Nebraska, 1971

Career: **149** by Rich Sanger (in 162 attempts)
Nebraska, 1971

Percentage
Season: **100%** Dana Coin (54 of 54)
Michigan, 1971

100%, Uwe Von Schamann (47 of 47)
Oklahoma, 1977

100%, Vince Petrucci (46 of 46)
Fresno State, 1977

Career: **97.3%**, Steve Robbins (108 of 111)
Washington, 1974–1977

97.0%, Carson Long (127-131)
Pittsburgh, 1973–1976

Consecutive

Game: **12** by Chuck Diedrick
Washington State, 1975

Season: **54** by Dana Coin
Michigan, 1971

Career: **87** by Don Bitterlich
Temple, 1973–1975

PROFESSIONAL
Most

Season: **61** by George Blanda (in 64 attempts)
Houston, 1961

Career: **943** by George Blanda
Chicago-Houston-Oakland, 1949–1975

Percentage

Career: **98%** by Ben Agajanian (199 of 204),
Numerous teams 1945–1964

Consecutive

234 by Tommy Davis
San Francisco

Field Goals

COLLEGE
Most

Game: **6** by Vince Fusco (in 7 attempts)
Duke, 1976

6 by Frank Nester (in 7 attempts)
West Virginia, 1972

6 by Charley Gogolak (in 6 attempts)
Princeton, 1965

Season: **21** by Don Bitterlich (in 31 attempts)
Temple, 1975

Career: **53** by Steve Little (in 89 attempts)
Arkansas, 1974–1977

Percentage
Game: **100%,** Charley Gogolak (6 of 6)
Princeton, 1965

Season: **83.3%,** Craig Jones (15 of 18)
VMI, 1976

77.3% Gerald Warren (17 of 22)
North Carolina State, 1967

Career: **73.2%,** Bob Berg (41 of 56)
New Mexico, 1973–1975

Consecutive
16 by Ishmael Ordonez
University of Arkansas, 1979

Longest Average
Game: **54.7 yards,** Clark Kimble (3: 63, 54, 47)
Colorado State, 1975

44.5 yards, Rod Garcia (4: 59, 52, 42, 25)
Stanford, 1973

Season: **48.3 yards,** Russell Erxelben (14)
Texas, 1977

Career: **38.9 yards,** Rafael Septien (32)
Southwest Louisiana, 1974–1976 ˙

Longest
67 yards, Steve Little
Arkansas, 1977

67 yards, Russell Erxelben
Texas, 1977

PROFESSIONAL
Most
Game: **7,** Jim Bakken (in 9 attempts)
St. Louis, 1967

Season: **34** by Jim Turner
New York Jets, 1968–1969

Career: **335,** George Blanda
Chicago-Houston-Oakland, 1949–1975

Percentage
Season: **88.5%,** Lou Groza (23 of 26)
Cleveland, 1953

Consecutive
        20, Garo Yepremian
Miami–New Orleans, 1978

Longest
        63 yards, Tom Dempsey
New Orleans, 1970

Punting

COLLEGE
Longest Average
Game: **57.2 yards,** Zack Jordan (6)
Colorado, 1950

          53.6 yards, Jack Benien (10)
Oklahoma State, 1971

Season: **49.3 yards,** Kirk Wilson (30)
          UCLA, 1956

          48.1 yards, Marv Bateman (68)
          Utah, 1971

Career: **46.9 yards,** Marv Bateman (133)
          Utah, 1970–1971

Longest:

          83 yards, Jerry Andrewlavage
          Colgate

          83 yards, Carl Birdsong
          West Texas State

PROFESSIONAL
Longest Average
Season: **51.3 yards,** Sam Baugh
          Washington, 1940

Career: **45.1 yards,** Sam Baugh
          Washington, 1937–1952

Longest

          96 yards, Steve O'Neal
          New York Jets, 1969

Photo Credits

NFL Properties: Pp. 10 (Paul Fine), 13, 33 (Dave Boss), 35-37, 38 (Malcolm W. Emmons), 39, 40 (Arthur Anderson), 41 (James Flores), 50 and 55 (Tak Makita), 69 (Dave Boss), 80 (Russ Reed).

David Burkett, Contact Press, New York, NY: Pp. 48-49, 59-62, 70-76

Tom Hoag, Long Beach, California: Pages 57, 64-67

Northwest Arkansas Times: Pages 24, 58

Citizens' Savings Sports Hall of Fame: Page 53